Why Brownlee Left

Acc

D0794993

also by Paul Muldoon

NEW WEATHER

MULES

Why Brownlee Left

PAUL MULDOON

FABER & FABER · London and Boston

First published in 1980
by Faber and Faber Limited
3 Queen Square London WC1N 3AU
Printed in Great Britain by
Bowering Press Ltd., Plymouth and London
All rights reserved

Conditions of Sale

British Library Cataloguing in Publication Data

Muldoon, Paul
    Why Brownlee left
    I. Title
    821'.9'14   PR6063.U367W/

ISBN 0-571-11592-6

Contents

FOR MICHAEL ALLEN

Whim

She was sitting with a pint and a small one
That afternoon in the Europa Hotel,
Poring over one of those old legends—
Cu Chulainn and the Birds of Appetite—
When he happened along, and took a pew.

'Pardon me, for I couldn't help but notice
You've got the O'Grady translation.'
'What of it? What's it to you?'
'Standish O'Grady? Very old-fashioned.
Cu Chulainn and the Birds of Appetite?
More like *How Cu Chulainn Got His End*.'
He smiled. She was smiling too.
'If you want the flavour of the original
You should be looking to Kuno Meyer.
As it happens, I've got the very edition
That includes this particular tale.
You could have it on loan, if you like,
If you'd like to call back to my place, now.'

Not that they made it as far as his place.
They would saunter through the Botanic Gardens
Where they held hands, and kissed,
And by and by one thing led to another.
To cut not a very long story short,

Once he got stuck into her he got stuck
Full stop.

They lay there quietly until dusk
When an attendant found them out.
He called an ambulance, and gently but firmly
They were manhandled on to a stretcher
Like the last of an endangered species.

October 1950

Whatever it is, it all comes down to this;
My father's cock
Between my mother's thighs.
Might he have forgotten to wind the clock?

Cookers and eaters, Fuck the Pope,
Wow and flutter, a one-legged howl,
My sly quadroon, the way home from the pub—
Anything wild or wonderful—

Whatever it is, it goes back to this night,
To a chance remark
In a room at the top of the stairs;
To an open field, as like as not,
Under the little stars.
Whatever it is, it leaves me in the dark.

The Geography Lesson

You should have seen them, small and wild
Against a map of the known world,

The back row of the class of '61.
Internal exiles at thirteen or fourteen.

Most couldn't read, though Mungo Park
Could write his name. He'd made his mark

As surely as some old explorer
Would christen a mountain, or a river.

To chart his progress, bench by embellished bench,
Till he petered out next to Lefty Lynch

Who kept ladybirds in a match-box,
Some with two, others with seven spots.

Who knew it all. Where to listen for the cuckoo
When she touched down from Africa.

Why bananas were harvested while green
But would hanker after where they'd grown,

Their sighing from the depths of a ship
Or from under the counter in Lightbody's shop,

How all that greenness turned to gold
Through unremembering darkness, an unsteady hold.

The Weepies

Most Saturday afternoons
At the local Hippodrome
Saw the Pathe-News rooster,
Then the recurring dream

Of a lonesome drifter
Through uninterrupted range.
Will Hunter, so gifted
He could peel an orange

In a single, fluent gesture,
Was the leader of our gang.
The curtain rose this afternoon
On a lion, not a gong.

When the crippled girl
Who wanted to be a dancer
Met the married man
Who was dying of cancer,

Our hankies unfurled
Like flags of surrender.
I believe something fell asunder
In even Will Hunter's hands.

Bran

While he looks into the eyes of women
Who have let themselves go,
While they sigh and they moan
For pure joy,

He weeps for the boy on that small farm
Who takes an oatmeal Labrador
In his arms,
Who knows all there is of rapture.

Cuba

My eldest sister arrived home that morning
In her white muslin evening dress.
'Who the hell do you think you are,
Running out to dances in next to nothing?
As though we hadn't enough bother
With the world at war, if not at an end.'
My father was pounding the breakfast-table.

'Those Yankees were touch and go as it was—
If you'd heard Patton in Armagh—
But this Kennedy's nearly an Irishman
So he's not much better than ourselves.
And him with only to say the word.
If you've got anything on your mind
Maybe you should make your peace with God.'

I could hear May from beyond the curtain.
'Bless me, Father, for I have sinned.
I told a lie once, I was disobedient once.
And, Father, a boy touched me once.'
'Tell me, child. Was this touch immodest?
Did he touch your breast, for example?'
'He brushed against me, Father. Very gently.'

The Bishop

The night before he was to be ordained
He packed a shirt and a safety razor
And started out for the middle of nowhere,
Back to the back of beyond,

Where all was forgiven and forgotten,
Or forgotten for a time. He would court
A childhood sweetheart.
He came into his uncle's fortune.

The years went by. He bought another farm of land.
His neighbours might give him a day
In the potatoes or barley.
He helped them with their tax demands.

There were children, who married
In their turn. His favourite grand-daughter
Would look out, one morning in January,
To find him in his armchair, in the yard.

It had snowed all night. There was a drift
As far as his chin, like an alb.
'Come in, my child. Come in, and bolt
The door behind you, for there's an awful draught.'

The Boundary Commission

You remember that village where the border ran
Down the middle of the street,
With the butcher and baker in different states?
Today he remarked how a shower of rain

Had stopped so cleanly across Golightly's lane
It might have been a wall of glass
That had toppled over. He stood there, for ages,
To wonder which side, if any, he should be on.

Early Warning

My father brought out his donkey-jacket,
Tipped a bucket
Of blue-stone into the knapsack sprayer,
A wing and a prayer
Against apple-scab disease,
And mizzled the lone crab-apple tree
In our back garden,
That was bowed down more by children
Than by any crop.

We would swing there on a fraying rope,
Lay siege to the tree-house,
Draw up our treaties
In its modest lee.

We would depend on more than we could see.

Our Protestant neighbour, Billy Wetherall,
Though he knew by the wireless
Of apple-scab in the air,
Would sling his hammock
Between two sturdy Grenadiers
And work through the latest *Marvel* comic.

Lull

I've heard it argued in some quarters
That in Armagh they mow the hay
With only a week to go to Christmas,
That no one's in a hurry

To save it, or their own sweet selves.
Tomorrow is another day,
As your man said on the Mount of Olives.
The same is held of County Derry.

Here and there up and down the country
There are still houses where the fire
Hasn't gone out in a century.

I know that eternal interim;
I think I know what they're waiting for
In Tyrone, Fermanagh, Down and Antrim.

I Remember Sir Alfred

The gardens of Buckingham Palace
Were strewn once with Irish loam
So those English moles that knew their place
Would have no sense of home.

Watching Irish navvies drinking pints
This evening in Camden Town
I remember Sir Alfred McAlpine—
The shortest distance between two points
Is a straight line.

The spirit of Sir Alfred McAlpine
Paces the meadow, and fixes his theodolite
On something beyond the horizon,
Love, or fidelity.

Charles Stewart Parnell, the I.R.A.,
Redheaded women, the way back to the digs,
The Irish squire
Who trained his spy-glass
On a distant spire
And imagined himself to be attending Mass.

Now Sir Alfred has dislodged a hare
That goes by leaps and bounds
Across the grazing,
Here and there,
This way and that, by singleminded swervings.

Ireland

The Volkswagen parked in the gap,
But gently ticking over.
You wonder if it's lovers
And not men hurrying back
Across two fields and a river.

Anseo

When the Master was calling the roll
At the primary school in Collegelands,
You were meant to call back *Anseo*
And raise your hand
As your name occurred.
Anseo, meaning here, here and now,
All present and correct,
Was the first word of Irish I spoke.
The last name on the ledger
Belonged to Joseph Mary Plunkett Ward
And was followed, as often as not,
By silence, knowing looks,
A nod and a wink, the Master's droll
'And where's our little Ward-of-court?'

I remember the first time he came back
The Master had sent him out
Along the hedges
To weigh up for himself and cut
A stick with which he would be beaten.
After a while, nothing was spoken;
He would arrive as a matter of course
With an ash-plant, a salley-rod.
Or, finally, the hazel-wand
He had whittled down to a whip-lash,
Its twist of red and yellow lacquers
Sanded and polished,
And altogether so delicately wrought
That he had engraved his initials on it.

I last met Joseph Mary Plunkett Ward
In a pub just over the Irish border.
He was living in the open,
In a secret camp
On the other side of the mountain.
He was fighting for Ireland,
Making things happen.
And he told me, Joe Ward,
Of how he had risen through the ranks
To Quartermaster, Commandant:
How every morning at parade
His volunteers would call back *Anseo*
And raise their hands
As their names occurred.

Why Brownlee Left

Why Brownlee left, and where he went,
Is a mystery even now.
For if a man should have been content
It was him; two acres of barley,
One of potatoes, four bullocks,
A milker, a slated farmhouse.
He was last seen going out to plough
On a March morning, bright and early.

By noon Brownlee was famous;
They had found all abandoned, with
The last rig unbroken, his pair of black
Horses, like man and wife,
Shifting their weight from foot to
Foot, and gazing into the future.

History

Where and when exactly did we first have sex?
Do you remember? Was it Fitzroy Avenue,
Or Cromwell Road, or Notting Hill?
Your place or mine? Marseilles or Aix?
Or as long ago as that Thursday evening
When you and I climbed through the bay window
On the ground floor of Aquinas Hall
And into the room where MacNeice wrote 'Snow',
Or the room where they say he wrote 'Snow'.

Palm Sunday

To tell the range of the English longbows
At Agincourt, or Crécy,
We need look no further than the yews
That, even in Irish graveyards,
Are bent on Fitzwilliams, and de Courcys.
These are the date-palms of the North.

They grow where nothing really should.
No matter how many are gathered
They never make a wood.
The coffin-board that yearns to be a tree
Goes on to bear no small, sweet gourds
As might be trampled by another Christ.

Today's the day for all such entrances.
I was wondering if you'd bring me through
To a world where everything stands
For itself, and carries
Just as much weight as me on you.
My scrawny door-mat. My deep, red carpet.

The Avenue

Now that we've come to the end
I've been trying to piece it together,
Not that distance makes anything clearer.
It began in the half-light
While we walked through the dawn chorus
After a party that lasted all night,
With the blackbird, the wood-pigeon,
The song-thrush taking a bludgeon
To a snail, our taking each other's hand
As if the whole world lay before us.

Something of a Departure

Would you be an angel
And let me rest,
This one last time,
Near that plum-coloured beauty spot
Just below your right buttock?

Elizabeth, Elizabeth,
Had words not escaped us both
I would have liked to hear you sing
Farewell to Tarwathie
Or *Ramble Away*.

Your thigh, your breast,
Your wrist, the ankle
That might yet sprout a wing—
You're altogether as slim
As the chance of our meeting again.

So put your best foot forward
And steady, steady on.
Show me the plum-coloured beauty spot
Just below your right buttock,
And take it like a man.

Holy Thursday

They're kindly here, to let us linger so late,
Long after the shutters are up.
A waiter glides from the kitchen with a plate
Of stew, or some thick soup,

And settles himself at the next table but one.
We know, you and I, that it's over,
That something or other has come between
Us, whatever we are, or were.

The waiter swabs his plate with bread
And drains what's left of his wine,
Then rearranges, one by one,
The knife, the fork, the spoon, the napkin,
The table itself, the chair he's simply borrowed,
And smiles, and bows to his own absence.

Making the Move

When Ulysses braved the wine-dark sea
He left his bow with Penelope,

Who would bend for no one but himself.
I edge along the book-shelf,

Past bad Lord Byron, Raymond Chandler,
Howard Hughes; The Hidden Years,

Past Blaise Pascal, who, bound in hide,
Divined the void to his left side :

Such books as one may think one owns
Unloose themselves like stones

And clatter down into this wider gulf
Between myself and my good wife;

A primus stove, a sleeping-bag,
The bow I bought through a catalogue

When I was thirteen or fourteen
That would bend, and break, for anyone,

Its boyish length of maple upon maple
Unseasoned and unsupple.

Were I embarking on that wine-dark sea
I would bring my bow along with me.

The Princess and the Pea

This is no dream
By Dulac out of the Brothers Grimm,
A child's disquiet,
Her impish mouth,
The quilt upon embroidered quilt
Of satin and shot silk,
Her lying there, extravagant, aloof,
Like cream on milk.

This is the dream of her older sister,
Who is stretched on the open grave
Of all the men she has known.
Far down, something niggles. The stir
Of someone still alive.
Then a cry, far down. It is your own.

Grief

If I think at all of the broken-down hearse
In the yard off the Moy square,
I think of a high-stepping, black horse
Stopped in mid-stride
Half-way up, say, Charlemont Street;
The immediate family looking on in horror.

He jolts to his knees on the kidney-stones
Where a frenzy of maggots
Make short work of so much blood and guts.
The hearse hasn't even been uncoupled.
His luminous, blue-pink skeleton
Simply disintegrates.

Till there's nothing left of our black horse
But the plume of his ornamental harness,
A tendril, a frond
Wavering among the cobbles;
The immediate family, and the family friends,
Leafing through their Bibles.

Come into My Parlour

When someone died, for miles around,
You were sure to find Coulter
In the graveyard at Collegelands
With his spade and navvy's shovel.
Once a plane broke up in mid-air
And he collected the bits and pieces,
A pocket-watch, a monocle,
As if all should come as second nature
To one who has strayed no farther
Than a ripple from its stone.

What Coulter took as his text
Was this bumpy half-acre of common.
Few graves were named or numbered
For most were family plots.
If the family had itself lost track
He knew exactly which was which
And what was what,
Where among the heights and hollows
Were the Quinns, and the O'Briens.

'I've been at the burying
Of so many of the Souper McAuleys
I declare they must be stacked
As high as dinner-plates.
Mind you, this ground's so wet
They're away again like snow off a ditch.
Them, and the best of good timber
Are come into the kingdom.'

And I saw over his tilting shoulder
The grave of my mother,
My father's grave, and his father's;
The slightly different level
Of the next field, and the next;
Each small, one-sided collision
Where a neighbour had met his future.
Here an O'Hara, there a Quinn,
The wreckage of bath-tubs and bedsteads,
Of couches and mangles,
That was scattered for miles around.

The One Desire

The palm-house in Belfast's Botanic Gardens
Was built before Kew
In the spirit that means to outdo
The modern by the more modern,

That iron be beaten, and glass
Bent to our will,
That heaven be brought closer still
And we converse with the angels.

The palm-house has now run to seed;
Rusting girders, a missing pane
Through which some delicate tree
Led by kindly light
Would seem at last to have broken through.
We have excelled ourselves again.

Immram

I was fairly and squarely behind the eight
That morning in Foster's pool-hall
When it came to me out of the blue
In the shape of a sixteen-ounce billiard cue
That lent what he said some little weight.
'Your old man was an ass-hole.
That makes an ass-hole out of you.'
My grand-father hailed from New York State.
My grand-mother was part Cree.
This must be some new strain in my pedigree.

The billiard-player had been big, and black,
Dressed to kill, or inflict a wound,
And had hung around the pin-table
As long as it took to smoke a panatella.
I was clinging to an ice-pack
On which the Titanic might have foundered
When I was suddenly bedazzled
By a little silver knick-knack
That must have fallen from his hat-band.
I am telling this exactly as it happened.

I suppose that I should have called the cops
Or called it a day and gone home
And done myself, and you, a favour.
But I wanted to know more about my father.
So I drove west to Paradise
Where I was greeted by the distant hum
Of Shall We Gather at the River?
The perfect introduction to the kind of place
Where people go to end their lives.
It might have been Bringing In the Sheaves.

My mother had just been fed by force,
A pint of lukewarm water through a rubber hose.
I hadn't seen her in six months or a year,
Not since my father had disappeared.
Now she'd taken an overdose
Of alcohol and barbiturates,
And this, I learned, was her third.
I was told then by a male nurse
That if I came back at the end of the week
She might be able to bring herself to speak.

Which brought me round to the Atlantic Club.
The Atlantic Club was an old grain-silo
That gave onto the wharf.
Not the kind of place you took your wife
Unless she had it in mind to strip
Or you had a mind to put her up for sale.
I knew how my father had come here by himself
And maybe thrown a little crap
And watched his check double, and treble,
With highball hard on the heels of highball.

She was wearing what looked like a dead fox
Over a low-cut sequinned gown,
And went by the name of Susan, or Suzanne.
A girl who would never pass out of fashion
So long as there's an 'if' in California.
I stood her one or two pink gins
And the talk might have come round to passion
Had it not been for a pair of thugs
Who suggested that we both take a wander,
She upstairs, I into the wild, blue yonder.

They came bearing down on me out of nowhere.
A Buick and a Chevrolet.
They were heading towards a grand slam.
Salami on rye. I was the salami.
So much for my faith in human nature.
The age of chivalry how are you?
But I side-stepped them, neatly as Salome,
So they came up against one another
In a moment of intense heat and light,
Like a couple of turtles on their wedding-night.

Both were dead. Of that I was almost certain.
When I looked into their eyes
I sensed the import of their recent visions,
How you must get all of wisdom
As you pass through a wind-shield.
One's frizzled hair was dyed
A peroxide blond, his sinewy arms emblazoned
With tattoos, his vest marked *Urgent*.
All this was taking on a shape
That might be clearer after a night's sleep.

When the only thing I had ever held in common
With anyone else in the world
Was the ramshackle house on Central Boulevard
That I shared with my child-bride
Until she dropped out to join a commune,
You can imagine how little I was troubled
To kiss Goodbye to its weathered clapboard.
When I nudged the rocker on the porch
It rocked as though it might never rest.
It seemed that I would forever be driving west.

I was in luck. She'd woken from her slumbers
And was sitting out among flowering shrubs.
All might have been peace and harmony
In that land of milk and honey
But for the fact that our days are numbered,
But for Foster's, the Atlantic Club,
And now, that my father owed Redpath money.
Redpath. She told me how his empire
Ran a little more than half-way to Hell
But began on the top floor of the Park Hotel.

Steel and glass were held in creative tension
That afternoon in the Park.
I strode through the cavernous lobby
And found myself behind a nervous couple
Who registered as Mr and Mrs Alfred Tennyson.
The unsmiling, balding desk-clerk
Looked like a man who would sell an alibi
To King Kong on tht Empire State building,
So I thought better of passing the time of day.
I took the elevator all the way.

You remember how, in a half-remembered dream,
You found yourself in a long corridor,
How behind the first door there was nothing,
Nothing behind the second,
Then how you swayed from room to empty room
Until, beyond that last half-open door
You heard a telephone . . . and you were wakened
By a woman's voice asking you to come
To the Atlantic Club, between six and seven,
And when you came, to come alone.

I was met, not by the face behind the voice,
But by yet another aide-de-camp
Who would have passed for a Barbary pirate
With a line in small-talk like a parrot
And who ferried me past an outer office
To a not ungracious inner sanctum.
I did a breast-stroke through the carpet,
Went under once, only to surface
Alongside the raft of a banquet-table—
A whole roast pig, its mouth fixed on an apple.

Beyond the wall-length, two-way mirror
There was still more to feast your eyes upon
As Susan, or Susannah, danced
Before what looked like an invited audience,
A select band of admirers
To whom she would lay herself open.
I was staring into the middle distance
Where two men and a dog were mowing her meadow
When I was hit by a hypodermic syringe.
And I entered a world equally rich and strange.

There was one who can only have been asleep
Among row upon row of sheeted cadavers
In what might have been the Morgue
Of all the cities of America,
Who beckoned me towards her slab
And silently drew back the covers
On the vermilion omega
Where she had been repeatedly stabbed,
Whom I would carry over the threshold of pain
That she might come and come and come again.

I came to, under a steaming pile of trash
In the narrow alley-way
Behind that old Deep Water Baptist mission
Near the corner of Sixteenth and Ocean—
A blue-eyed boy, the Word made flesh
Amid no hosannahs nor hallelujahs
But the strains of Blind Lemon Jefferson
That leaked from the church
Through a hole in a tiny, stained-glass window,
In what was now a torrent, now had dwindled.

And honking to Blind Lemon's blues guitar
Was a solitary, black cat
Who would have turned the heads of Harlem.
He was no louder than a fire-alarm,
A full-length coat of alligator,
An ermine stole, his wide-brimmed hat
Festooned with family heirlooms.
I watch him trickle a fine, white powder
Into his palm, so not a grain would spill,
Then snort it through a rolled-up dollar bill.

This was angel dust, dust from an angel's wing
Where it glanced off the land of cocaine,
Be that Bolivia, Peru.
Or snow from the slopes of the Andes, so pure
It would never melt in spring.
But you know how over every Caliban
There's Ariel, and behind him, Prospero;
Everyone taking a cut, dividing and conquering
With lactose and dextrose,
Everyone getting right up everyone else's nose.

I would tip-toe round by the side of the church
For a better view. Some fresh cement.
I trod as lightly there
As a mere mortal at Grauman's Chinese Theatre.
An oxy-acetylene torch.
There were two false-bottomed
Station-waggons. I watched Mr See-You-Later
Unload a dozen polythene packs
From one to the other. *The Urgent Shipping Company*.
It behoved me to talk to the local P.D.

'My father, God rest him, he held this theory
That the Irish, the American Irish,
Were really the thirteenth tribe,
The Israelites of Europe.
All along, my father believed in fairies
But he might as well have been Jewish.'
His laugh was a slight hiccup.
I guessed that Lieutenant Brendan O'Leary's
Grand-mother's pee was green,
And that was why she had to leave old Skibbereen.

Now, what was all this about the Atlantic cabaret,
Urgent, the top floor of the Park?
When had I taken it into my head
That somebody somewhere wanted to see me dead?
Who? No, Redpath was strictly on the level.
So why, rather than drag in the Narcs.,
Why didn't he and I drive over to Ocean Boulevard
At Eighteenth Street, or wherever?
Would I mind stepping outside while he made a call
To such-and-such a luminary at City Hall?

We counted thirty-odd of those brown-eyed girls
Who ought to be in pictures,
Bronzed, bleached, bare-breasted,
Bare-assed to a man,
All sitting, cross-legged, in a circle
At the feet of this life-guard out of Big Sur
Who made an exhibition
Of his dorsals and his pectorals
While one by one his disciples took up the chant
The Lord is my surf-board. I shall not want.

He went on to explain to O'Leary and myself
How only that morning he had acquired the lease
On the old Baptist mission,
Though his was a wholly new religion.
He called it *The Way Of The One Wave.*
This one wave was sky-high, like a wall of glass,
And had come to him in a vision.
You could ride it forever, effortlessly.
The Lieutenant was squatting before his new guru.
I would inform the Missing Persons Bureau.

His name? I already told you his name.
Forty-nine. Fifty come July.
Five ten or eleven. One hundred and eighty pounds.
He could be almost anyone.
And only now was it brought home to me
How rarely I looked in his eyes,
Which were hazel. His hair was mahogany brown.
There was a scar on his left forearm
From that time he got himself caught in the works
Of a saw-mill near Ithaca, New York.

I was just about getting things into perspective
When a mile-long white Cadillac
Came sweeping out of the distant past
Like a wayward Bay mist,
A transport of joy. There was that chauffeur
From the 1931 Sears Roebuck catalogue,
Susannah, as you guessed,
And this refugee from F. Scott Fitzgerald
Who looked as if he might indeed own the world.
His name was James Earl Caulfield III.

This was how it was. My father had been a mule.
He had flown down to Rio
Time and time again. But he courted disaster.
He tried to smuggle a wooden statue
Through the airport at Lima.
The Christ of the Andes. The statue was hollow.
He stumbled. It went and shattered.
And he had to stand idly by
As a cool fifty or sixty thousand dollars worth
Was trampled back into the good earth.

He would flee, to La Paz, then to Buenos Aires,
From alias to alias.
I imagined him sitting outside a hacienda
Somewhere in the Argentine.
He would peer for hours
Into the vastness of the pampas.
Or he might be pointing out the constellations
Of the Southern hemisphere
To the open-mouthed child at his elbow.
He sleeps with a loaded pistol under his pillow.

The mile-long white Cadillac had now wrapped
Itself round the Park Hotel.
We were spirited to the nineteenth floor
Where Caulfield located a secret door.
We climbed two perilous flights of steps
To the exclusive penthouse suite.
A moment later I was ushered
Into a chamber sealed with black drapes.
As I grew accustomed to the gloom
I realized there was someone else in the room.

He was huddled on an old orthopaedic mattress,
The makings of a skeleton,
Naked but for a pair of draw-string shorts.
His hair was waistlength, as was his beard.
He was covered in bedsores.
He raised one talon.
'I forgive you,' he croaked. 'And I forget.
On your way out, you tell that bastard
To bring me a dish of ice-cream.
I want Baskin-Robbins banana-nut ice-cream.'

I shimmied about the cavernous lobby.
Mr and Mrs Alfred Tennyson
Were ahead of me through the revolving door.
She tipped the bell-hop five dollars.
There was a steady stream of people
That flowed in one direction,
Faster and deeper,
That I would go along with, happily,
As I made my way back, like any other pilgrim,
To Main Street, to Foster's pool-room.

Acknowledgements

Acknowledgements are due to the editors of :
*The First Ten Years, Fortnight, Honest Ulsterman,
Listener, London Review of Books, New Irish Writing,
Poetry Review, Poetry Society Supplement* (Christmas
1979), *A Sense of Ireland, Stand* and *Stone Ferry Review*;
to BBC 2, Radio 3 and Radio Eireann.

I am indebted to Whitley Stokes's translation of
'Immram Mael Duin' (*Revue Celtique* IX-X).

I also gratefully acknowledge the assistance of the
Arts Council of Great Britain.